What's New
At The Zoo?

written by Sharon Fear   illustrated by Adrienne Kennaway

HARCOURT BRACE & COMPANY

Orlando   Atlanta   Austin   Boston   San Francisco   Chicago   Dallas   New York
Toronto   London

Something was happening at the zoo.

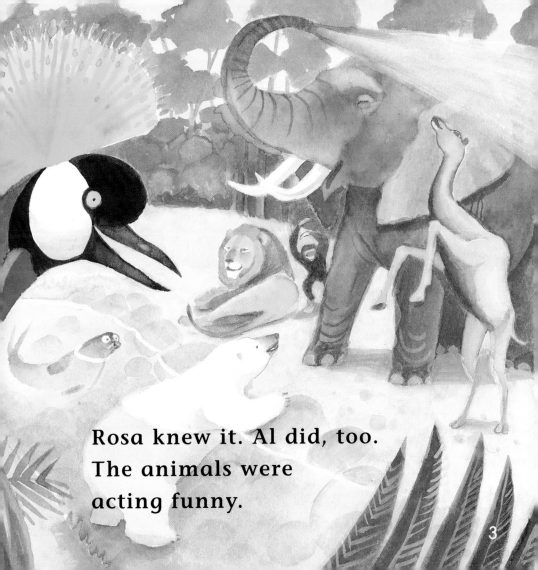

Rosa knew it. Al did, too.
The animals were
acting funny.

3

The chimp was in the lion's cage.

The seal was swimming
with the polar bear.

The camel was talking to the elephant. Rosa tried to hear what they were saying, but they were whispering!

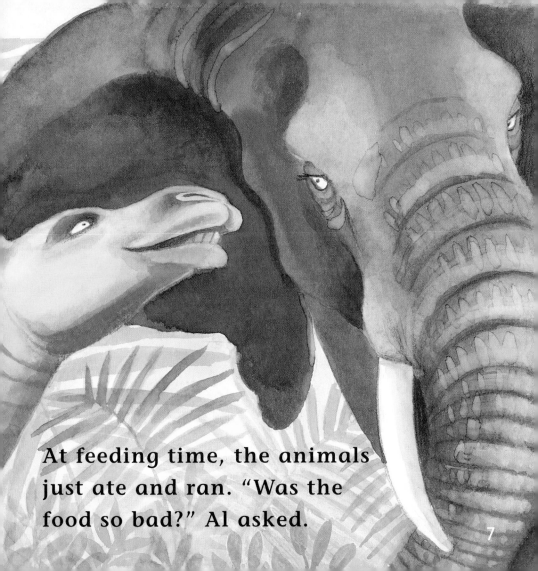

At feeding time, the animals just ate and ran. "Was the food so bad?" Al asked.

At bath time, the animals just got wet and hurried away. "Was the water too cold?" Rosa asked.

9

Al and Rosa tried hard to please.
"Would you like some sweet hay?"
asked Rosa.

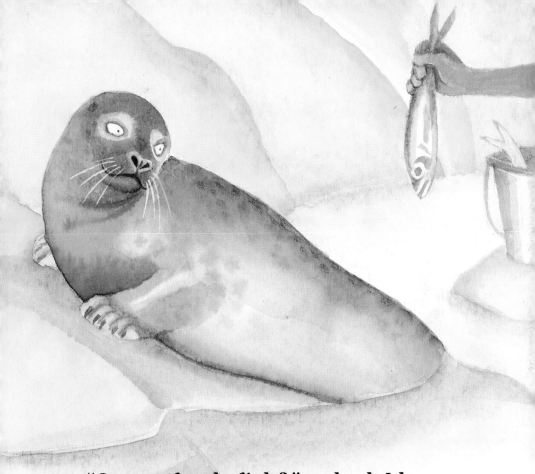

"Some fresh fish?" asked Al.

But all the animals just turned away.

13

"What IS the trouble?" cried Al.
"There is the trouble," said Rosa.

14

Al and Rosa ran over and took a peek.
There was no trouble at the zoo.
Something new arrived at the zoo.

Oh! What a pretty baby!